LOVE DIVINE

A COLLECTION OF VICTORIAN & EDWARDIAN ANTHEMS

FOR MIXED VOICE CHOIRS
SELECTED & EDITED BY BARRY ROSE

D1209145

NOVELLO

FRONT COVER St. Augustine's Church, Kilburn, London, courtesy Paul Barker/
Country Life Picture Library
BACK COVER photograph of Barry Rose by Timothy Hands

COVER DESIGN Fresh Lemon

MUSIC SETTING Barnes Music Engraving

NOV032208
ISBN 1-84449-683-X

HEAD OFFICE
8/9 Frith Street,
London W1D 3JB
England
Tel +44 (0)20 7434 0066
Fax +44 (0)20 7287 6329

SALES AND HIRE
Music Sales Limited,
Newmarket Road,
Bury St Edmunds,
Suffolk IP33 3YB
England
Tel +44 (0)1284 702600
Fax +44 (0)1284 768301

www.chesternovello.com
e-mail: music@musicsales.co.uk

Other anthologies by Barry Rose available from Novello:

High Praise NOV032118
High Praise 2 NOV020680
Merrily on High NOV032121
More than Hymns 1 NOV040043
More than Hymns 2 NOV040044
More than Psalms NOV040062
Sing Low NOV381000

Contents

Introduction

Music in church has always been a reflection of the liturgical practices of the time, and there is, perhaps, no period of which this is truer than the Victorian and Edwardian eras.

It was during the early years of Queen Victoria's reign that organs and robed choirs were first introduced into the chancels of our parish churches, and they needed new and accessible music as anthems, as well as some settings of the Canticles for Morning and Evening Prayer. Also influential was the new order brought into worship through the influence of the Oxford (Tractarian) Movement, resulting in many spectacularly grand buildings which we still cherish today.

This collection sets out to bring you a flavour of anthems and settings from those times. Mainly using scriptural and hymn texts, the music is melodious and harmonically logical, written with a sincerity and fervour, reflecting the forms of worship with which the composers worked. Anthems for church choirs are juxtaposed against larger scale settings of the Canticles, written by cathedral and collegiate organists for their own choirs.

We hope that the explanatory notes will help to set each of the pieces into some sort of historical context, and I would like to thank Elizabeth Robinson for her advice and help in every aspect of the preparation of this volume.

Barry Rose
Somerset, January 2005

Notes on the music

Charles Villiers Stanford · And I saw another angel

One of Stanford's less frequently sung anthems, the text is from the Epistle at Holy Communion on All Saints' Day, as appointed in the 1662 Book of Common Prayer. The music dates from 1885, whilst the composer was organist at Trinity College, Cambridge, and may have been written for his own chapel choir to sing.

With typical musical craftsmanship, Stanford sets the opening mood of the text with some ethereally angelic high chords on the organ, leading to the narration from a solo tenor, and answered by the basses (bar 22) with the organ playing solemn fanfare-like interspersions. If there is a key word here, it must surely be *drama*, especially in the two similar choruses 'And lo, a great multitude' and 'blessing and glory', and it is here that the basic tempo may need to have more of a sense of urgency.

In a piece which can truly be described as episodic, the art of the successful performance is to make the musical joins sound seamless as one tempo change unobtrusively melts into the next. Although Stanford did not provide any metronome markings, I suggest that the opening should be ♩ = 82, bars 22 to 32 ♩ = 92, and the choruses (bars 33 and 98) ♩ = 120.

Charles Villiers Stanford · Benedictus in G

Written in 1904, Stanford's Morning and Evening Canticles in G followed on from his already well-known settings in A, B flat and C. The *Benedictus* is part of the Office of Morning Prayer in the 1662 Book of Common Prayer, where it is appointed to be sung after the second lesson. The text comes from St. Luke, Chapter 1, and is part of the narrative telling of the birth of John the Baptist.

In musical terms, it is not an easy text to set, but Stanford makes light of this, from an assured and positive opening phrase sung by the lower voices, to the extraordinary moments of tenderness and calm sung by the full choir at 'that we being delivered...' and 'to guide our feet into the way of peace'. Every musical mood he creates reflects the true meaning of the words – the hallmark of the finest choral composers – and the whole work achieves a complete musical unity, finishing with the well-known Gloria, also used in the Magnificat in G. Although Morning Prayer is not often sung chorally nowadays, this setting makes an ideal concert or recital item.

Henry Balfour Gardiner · Evening Hymn

Promoter of concerts and champion of English music, Henry Balfour Gardiner studied composition in Frankfurt, where he was greatly influenced by the music of Wagner and Tchaikovsky. The *Evening Hymn*, a setting of a text used in the Office of Compline, has long been a favourite with choirs. After the initial build up in the organ introduction, the first choral entry makes a great impact on the listener, even if the writing does not totally reflect the spirit of the words – a prayer in the quiet of evening! The mood is better caught in the quieter middle section, with its chromatic progressions depicting 'nightly fears and fantasies', though it is here that tuning can be a problem, and many a choir has shown great surprise (and disappointment) when the organ has re-entered at bar 55 in what seems to be another key! The mood of the text is well caught by the last verse, and the extended *Amen* shows all the dramatic effects of operatic influence, with its hushed and sustained ending. Musical unity is achieved as the piece ends with the single pedal note on the organ with which it began.

Edward Elgar · How calmly the evening

Elgar's setting dates from 1907, the year in which he celebrated his 50th birthday and wrote the first of the *Wand of Youth* Suites. Originally published as an insert in *The Musical Times*, he used a text from *Thoughts on a Day*, a collection of poems by T.T. Lynch, first published in 1844. Thomas Toke Lynch was a congregational minister in London, and also a musician and poet. He was dogged by ill health throughout his life, and some of the words of his poem ('we come to be soothed with thy merciful healing...') may well have been a reflection on his own state of body and mind.

The music bears the hallmarks of the composer's inimitably gracious melodic lines, and as with so much of his music, the key words for your choir should be *musical ebb and flow within the phrases*, if the interpretation is to avoid sounding four-square.

John Stainer · I am Alpha and Omega

Through the regular readings at matins and evensong, the symbolism and imagery of the Book of Revelation would have been well known to John Stainer, and his bold organ introduction effectively paints the powerful statement in verse 8 of the first chapter – I am Alpha and Omega. Stainer had been appointed organist of St. Paul's Cathedral in 1872, and his many compositions show an understanding of the cathedral's 7-second reverberation, sometimes with pauses written in over the rests (see bars 2 and 4), and tempi that might be considered stolid, but which ensured that the music and words were heard clearly by the congregation. The piece was written in 1878 and was published in *The Musical Times* in May that year.

In terms of structure, the music is apparently simple, but the effect of starting with just the basses, then adding the tenors, and the full choir, heightens the drama of the text. As in the well-known setting of *I saw the Lord*, there is a quieter section for treble or tenor solo (though this could well by sung by a semi-chorus of upper voices), which is mirrored by the choir in four-part harmony. The recurrence of the opening theme at bar 90 brings the piece to a suitably reverent and hushed ending. If there are key words to help your interpretation, they must surely be *drama* for pages 31 to 34, and *vocal warmth and commitment* from page 35 to the end.

Horatio Parker · Jam sol recedit

The American composer Horatio Parker studied composition with Josef Rheinberger, and later held appointments as organist at churches in New York and Boston. In 1897, whilst he was organist at Trinity Church, Boston, the Oratorio Society of New York commissioned him to write the dramatic oratorio *The Legend of St. Christopher*, from which this eight-part unaccompanied chorus is taken. The influence of his teacher can clearly be seen and heard in the dramatic and sometimes chromatic approach to the text, and the thrillingly opulent vocal climaxes help to highlight the contrast with the serene four-part writing at such places as 'Infunde lumen cordibus' (bar 20 onwards).

Later, Dean of the School of Music at Yale University, Parker became a teacher of composition techniques, and his understanding of word-painting can be seen in every phrase of this exciting piece – from the delicate falling opening phrase ('Now sinks the sun') to the declamatory repeated Glorias, and the extended and hushed Amen.

The English translation was made by his mother, Isabella Grahame Parker, though we recommend that it is sung in the original Latin text, and also in the key of G flat (see footnote on page 38).

F.A.G. Ouseley · Jerusalem on high

Born into an aristocratic family, Frederick Arthur Gore Ouseley was educated at Oxford University and ordained into the Church of England in 1849. He became a curate at St. Barnabas, Pimlico, London, where he funded a new organ, and financially supported the choir. This was the period of the Tractarian (Oxford) Movement, and in 1854, probably inspired by the musical reputation Samuel Sebastian Wesley was gaining at Leeds Parish Church, Ouseley set out to build and fund his own choral foundation – St. Michael's in Tenbury Wells, a small market-town in the county of Worcestershire. There he built a magnificent church, and an adjacent college to house and educate the choristers who sang the daily offices in the church. An accomplished organist and composer, Ouseley also became Professor of Music at Oxford University.

Jerusalem on high is a chorus from the oratorio *Hagar*, first performed in Hereford Cathedral in 1873 with full orchestral accompaniment. The text is based on the Old Testament story of Hagar, the Egyptian handmaid of Sarah, the wife of Abraham (Genesis 16), though the words of this hymn text are by a seventeenth-century dean of Bristol Cathedral, Samuel Crossman, and are part of a longer fourteen-stanza poem based on heaven – *Sweet place, sweet place alone*.

Heathcote Statham arranged the accompaniment for keyboard during his tenure as organist at St. Michael's, Tenbury, and *Jerusalem on high* was sung every year at the College's Michaelmas services. This piece can be sung too quickly, and a useful tip is to set the initial tempo by taking a comfortable speed for the semi-quavers from bar 52 onwards.

Edward Elgar · Light out of darkness

One of Elgar's most dramatic settings for choir – a chorus from his first oratorio *The Light of Life (Lux Christi)* – written in 1896, and first performed at the Three Choirs Festival in Worcester Cathedral that year. At that time, Edward Elgar was 39 and known only locally as a violin teacher and member of the orchestra at the Three Choirs Festivals, and the invitation to write a work for such a prestigious musical occasion offered him his first opportunity to write an extended choral and orchestral work.

For a text, he turned to a musical friend, Edward Capel Cure. Known by Elgar as a cellist in his chamber music group, the Reverend Edward Capel Cure had been ordained in Worcester Cathedral and had served his first curacy at Holy Trinity Church, Worcester. He used the ninth chapter of the Gospel according to St. John as the basis for his text – the miracle of Jesus healing the blind man – and gave the work its original title of *Lux Christi*.

From the very outset of the introduction to *Light out of darkness* there is agitated drama, soon punctuated by expectant sustained chords which may well depict the dawning of the blind man's sight. The first two chorus leads simply use the word *light*, in a mood of glorious exultation – you can almost hear it as a shout of thanksgiving for the miracle. There are many moods in this fine piece – drama and pathos are juxtaposed – and as with much of Elgar, the use of varying tempi and *rubato* (which Elgar often marked as *tenuto*) will help you and your choir to bring the words to life successfully.

Three years after it was written, a revised version of *The Light of Life* was performed at the 1899 Worcester Three Choirs Festival, by which time Elgar was nationally acclaimed, following his newest composition, the *Enigma Variations*.

Samuel Sebastian Wesley · The Lord is my shepherd

Probably the most influential church musician of the nineteenth century, Samuel Sebastian Wesley was organist of four cathedrals, Hereford (1832), Exeter (1835), Winchester (1849) and Gloucester (1865), as well as spending seven years at the then newly consecrated Leeds Parish Church (1842-49). An accomplished organist, choir trainer and composer, his choirs set a standard of attendance and behaviour at services which he vainly hoped cathedral deans and canons would follow. Never afraid to criticise the clergy, he soon made himself unpopular with them, and his own words neatly sum this up – 'if he (the organist) gives trouble in his attempts at improvement, he will be, by some Chapters (the Cathedral clergy), at once voted a person with whom they "cannot get along smoothly"....'.

Like so many composers, Wesley's music was written for the size and ability of choir with which he was working at the time. As with his well-known *Blessed be the God and Father*, this setting of Psalm 23 gives the solo passages to a bass and a treble, though these could be sung by a semi-chorus, or *tutti*. The different moods of the text are created through the use of varying tempi and time-signatures, and in the triple-time sections your choir will need to take care that there is a certain lightness in its singing – it always helps to think of these sections as having just the one strong beat (at the beginning of the bar).

The 'colours' painted by the different musical keys have long been a fascination to me, and it is interesting that Wesley chose the warmth and comfort of F major for this pastoral text, only moving into its darker relative D minor for 'Yea, though I walk through the valley of the shadow of death'. Was he influenced by the F major in which Beethoven begins his 'Pastoral' Symphony, and did the later Stanford setting of this same text (also in F major) follow Wesley's example?

John Stainer · Love divine! all loves excelling

A delightfully melodious duet for soprano and tenor from Stainer's oratorio *The Daughter of Jairus*, which was written for the 1878 Three Choirs Festival at Worcester Cathedral. Scored for choir, orchestra, soprano and tenor soloists, the oratorio relates the New Testament story of the death of the daughter of Jairus, one of the rulers of the synagogue, and the subsequent miracle of Jesus bringing her back to life.

In the oratorio, the narrative is given to a soprano soloist, whilst the tenor has an extended aria ('My hope is in the Everlasting'). Their duet appears just before the last chorus, and uses words from the well-known hymn by Charles Wesley in the abridged form by his brother John, as published in his 1780 *Collection of Hymns*. Stainer takes one liberty with the text – substituting 'hasten' for Wesley's 'suddenly' (bar 48), presumably on the grounds of better word stressing, and it may be as a direct result of this extended setting that he was persuaded to write his now well-known hymn tune *Love Divine* (in the same key), for the 1889 Supplement to *Hymns Ancient and Modern*.

John Goss · Magnificat & Nunc Dimittis in E

As a long serving organist of St. Paul's Cathedral (from 1838-72), John Goss is probably best remembered for his tunes to *Praise, my soul, the King of Heaven* and *See, amid the winter's snow*.

Despite having the musical resources associated with a great cathedral, the choir at St. Paul's at that time was quite small, and not of a high vocal or musical standard. This may explain why Goss wrote so much of his music in an apparently simple four-part style, though he did so with a melodic flair and musical assurance, immediately apparent in this setting of the canticles for the office of evensong. Written in 1854, the part-writing is not difficult, supported throughout by the organ, whilst the treble line is lovingly crafted, with flowing vocal lines and an innate understanding of the meaning of the text. First published in 1866, the composer did not indicate any metronome markings. As basic speeds, we suggest Magnificat ($\downarrow$ = 100) and Nunc Dimittis ($\downarrow$= 92).

John Goss · O pray for the peace of Jerusalem

A gentle and memorable setting of familiar words from Psalm 122, *O pray for the peace of Jerusalem* is the central section of the larger anthem *Praise the Lord, O my Soul*, specially written for the 200th Festival of the Sons of the Clergy, held in St. Paul's Cathedral on 10 May 1854. John Goss took his texts from three different psalms and scored the accompaniment for full orchestra, though the score and parts have since been lost.

In a service of ecclesiastical pomp and splendour, held in the great space under the dome, Goss's quiet and reflective music to *O pray for the peace of Jerusalem* would have brought some moments of prayerful calm, and that is very much the spirit in which it should be approached by performers. The music eloquently portrays the mood and meaning of the text, and the inspired key changes at both appearances of 'Peace be within thy walls' help to bring a special serenity and meaning to those words. Although the suggested metronome marking indicates a quaver (eighth note) beat, I suggest that the musical flow will be helped if singers, conductors and organists think in slow crotchet (quarter note) beats, where possible.

F.A.G. Ouseley · O Saviour of the world
With its use of eight-part writing, Ouseley's sonorous setting of *O Saviour of the world* is quite unusual at a time when choirs were often quite small. The text had become associated with the Maundy Thursday liturgies, and his work may have been written for one of these at St. Michael's, Tenbury. Just thirty bars in length, it has an intensity and inspirational quality rarely found in this period of music. Although often sung unaccompanied, it was originally intended to be supported by the organ, not only adding depth and sonority, but also providing the upbeat to the final phrase (bar 27).

George Macfarren · Remember me, O Lord
George Macfarren studied piano and trombone at the Royal Academy of Music in London, and at the age of 21, returned there as professor of harmony. Forty years later, in 1875, he was appointed Principal, having been elected Professor of Music at Cambridge University a year earlier. His work as a scholar included performing editions of Purcell's *Dido and Aeneas* and some Handel oratorios. This short anthem, *Remember me, O Lord*, was originally intended to be accompanied, presumably with the organ doubling the voice parts, since no separate accompaniment was included. We have added an independent organ part which can be abridged or amended at the player's discretion.

Felix Mendelssohn · See what love
A memorable short chorus from the oratorio *St. Paul*, the theme of which may well owe its inspiration to the composer's friendship with Thomas Attwood, then organist of St. Paul's Cathedral in London. Mendelssohn loved to visit St. Paul's and play the organ, and it is recorded that one Sunday afternoon in 1829, he played so long after the service that the virgers could not get the congregation to leave. In desperation, they instructed the man blowing the organ to let the air out in the middle of a Bach fugue!

St. Paul was completed early in 1836 (two years before Attwood's death), and was first performed in Düsseldorf on 22 May that year, an English text being provided later by the translator of some of his other works, William Bartholomew (1784-1869). Towards the end of his life, the apostle Paul leaves Ephesus to go to Jerusalem, telling his followers that they will see him no more (Acts 20, vv. 36 and 38); this short chorus is sung as their affirmation of their belief that they are indeed 'God's own children'. The composer provided a piano reduction of his orchestral accompaniment, but in view of the limited range of the organ keyboard, we have transposed some of the higher notes down an octave. Beautifully phrased *legato* lines from the singers will make an elegant contrast with the constantly moving accompaniment.

John Varley Roberts · Seek ye the Lord
Born and raised in the county of Yorkshire, John Varley Roberts became a church organist at the age of 12 and was later to establish a reputation as a legendary choir trainer. Having gained his Bachelor of Music at Oxford University in 1871, and a Doctorate in Music five years later, he returned to the university in 1882 as Organist and Informator Choristarum at Magdalen College, a post he held for the next thirty-seven years. Contemporary accounts describe long queues in Oxford's High Street (known as The High) waiting to attend evensong in Magdalen College Chapel, and his much admired approach to choir training was later encapsulated in his 1898 book *A Practical Method of Training Choristers*.

His setting of *Seek ye the Lord* has long been a favourite with choirs and shows Varley Roberts to be the master of easy flowing melodic lines, both in the vocal parts and the accompaniment. The key words to a committed performance are *affectionate singing* and *elegant phrasing*.

Joseph Barnby · Sweet is Thy mercy
Now best remembered for his many psalm chants and well-known hymn tunes, Joseph Barnby's introduction to church music was in 1845, as a chorister at York Minster. He then studied at the Royal Academy of Music and in 1863, became organist and choirmaster at the newly built church of St. Andrew's, Wells Street, London, where he founded a men's and boys' choir to rival, and even surpass, that at All Saints, Margaret Street, a few hundred yards away. In 1871, he moved to St. Anne's Church, Soho and later that year, conducted the first church performance in England of Bach's *St. Matthew Passion*, in Westminster Abbey. His later career took him to Eton College, as Precentor (Director

of Music) and to the Guildhall School of Music, as Principal.

Sweet is thy mercy is typical of his accessible style of writing and dates from his time at Eton. The text is one of over 300 hymns written by the Reverend John Samuel Monsell, then rector of St. Nicholas Church, Guildford, twenty miles from Eton. Although marked 'solo', it is possible for those passages to be sung by a semi-chorus, especially after the choir has begun singing (bar 20).

John W. Gritton · Teach me, O Lord

The eldest of ten children, John Gritton spent his working life in the county of Surrey, England, and was the first in a continuing line of musicians in the Gritton family. From 1887 until his death in 1928, he was organist and choirmaster at St. Mary's Parish Church, Reigate, where his son Eric later succeeded him. Whilst there, he and Godfrey Searle (a member of his choir), were jointly responsible for the maintenance of the boys' choir and provision of a property for their recreation and boarding, now Reigate St. Mary's School, where today's choristers are educated.

The text of *Teach me, O Lord* lends itself to triple time, and various composers have written settings in this metre. Whilst Gritton's music is typically melodic of the period, it also uses many chromatic passages which will need careful rehearsal and tuning by the lower parts in your choir.

Arthur Sullivan · Turn Thy face from my sins

Although inextricably linked with operetta through his librettist partner W.S.Gilbert, Arthur Sullivan also wrote large-scale orchestral and choral works, solo songs and several well-known hymn tunes, still in use today. He began composing whilst he was a boy chorister in the Chapel Royal at St. James's Palace, London, and his first anthem was published at the age of 13. In direct competition with Joseph Barnby, he became the first holder of the newly instituted Mendelssohn Scholarship, studied composition at the Royal Academy of Music in London, and continued his studies at the Leipzig Conservatory.

The Lenten setting of *Turn Thy face from my sins* was published in 1878 whilst Sullivan was Principal of the National Training School of Music in London. It is typical of the period with its use of block chords and chromatic progressions. Success in its interpretation will rely greatly on the attitude of your singers, who need to approach the music and text with sincerity, affection and expressive singing throughout.

Adolphe Adam · O holy night!

As the congregation assembled for midnight mass at Christmas 1847 in the village of Roquemaure in the Languedoc region of France, they could have had no idea that they were about to hear the first performance of a song, *Cantique de Noël*, which would later become world famous and remain a firm favourite with soloists and choirs. The composer was Adolphe Adam, then well-known in France for his operas and ballets and, in particular, the music to *Giselle*, composed in 1841. The local connection was through the poem *Minuit, Chrétien*, written by Placide Cappeau, a local wine merchant who was also the mayor of Roquemaure at that time.

Reactions to the work were divided, not least since the mayor was not often seen in church, and the local clergy resented the work of a Jewish composer being sung in their beautiful fourteenth-century building, criticising it for its 'lack of musical taste'. But time has shown that *Cantique de Noël* lives on, and seems to have gained an indestructible popularity since its translation into English by the American priest and music critic John Sullivan Dwight (1813-93).

In this well-known arrangement, for soloist and choir, we have altered some of Dwight's words to match the original French text. If it is being sung in English, soloists may find that the English words might flow more easily if the rhythm at the first vocal entry is changed to

Barry Rose

And I saw another angel

Revelation ch. 7, vv. 2–3, 9–10, 12

Charles Villiers Stanford (1852–1924)
Op. 37, No. 1

Tenor SOLO: And I saw a-no-ther an - gel as - cend- -ing from the east, hav-ing the seal of the liv - ing God;___ and he cried with a loud voice to the four an-gels, say - ing,

Solenne

B. (TUTTI)

Hurt not the earth, nei - ther the sea, nor the

Sw. with Reeds
8 ft. & 4 ft.

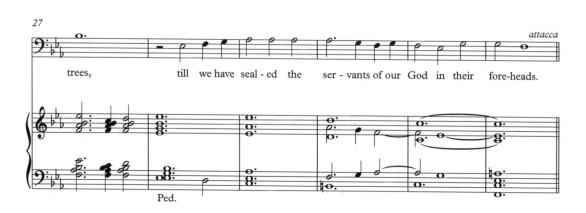

trees, till we have seal - ed the ser - vants of our God in their fore-heads.

Ped.

attacca

S.

And lo, a great mul - ti - tude,___

A.

And lo, a great mul - ti - tude,___ which

T. TUTTI

And lo, a great mul - ti - tude, which no man could

B.

And lo, a great mul - ti - tude,___ which___ no man could num -

Gt.

16 & 32 ft.

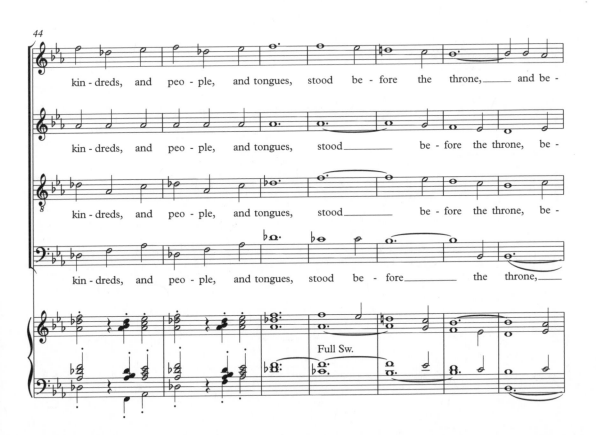

4

5

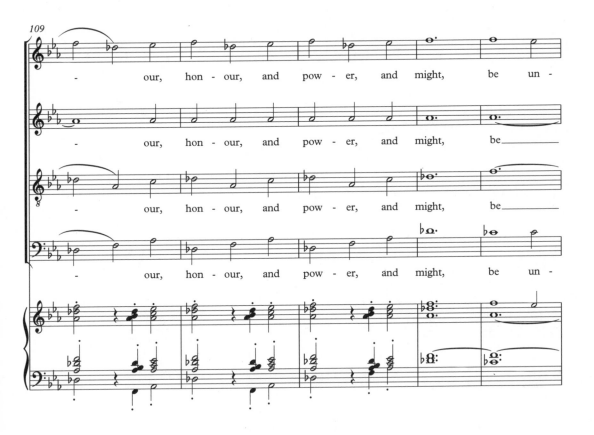

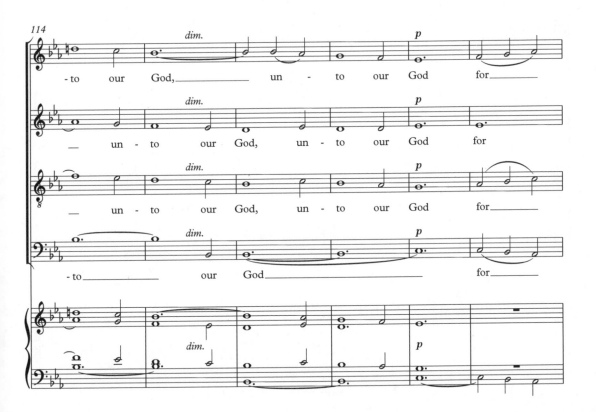

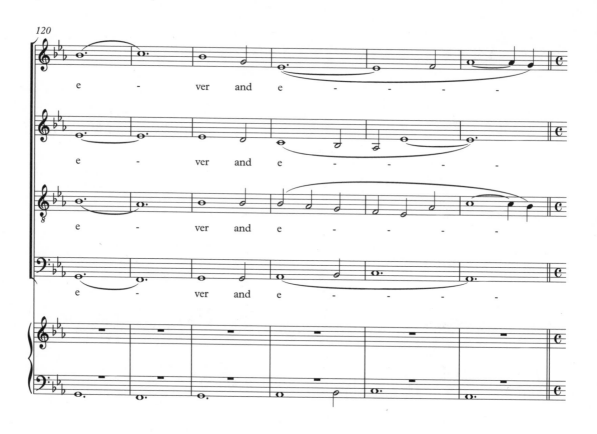

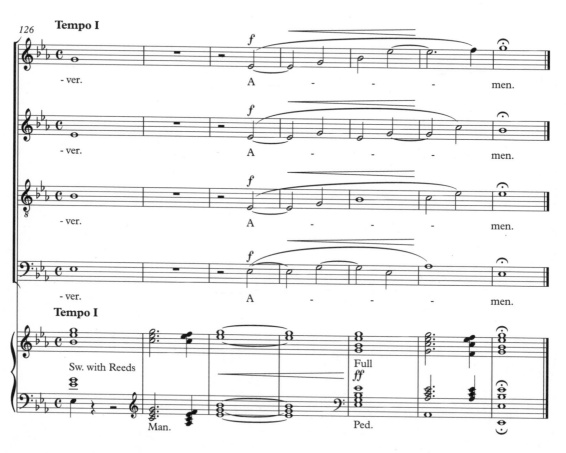

Benedictus in G

St. Luke ch. 1, vv. 68–79

Charles Villiers Stanford (1852–1924)
Op. 81

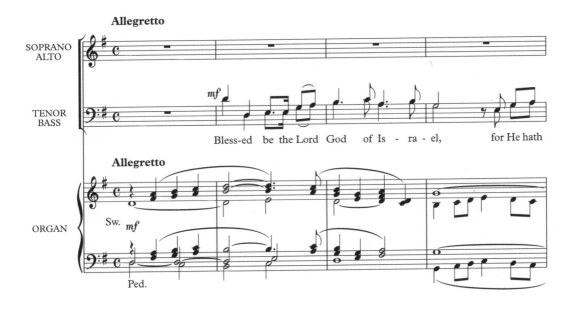

migh - ty sal - va - tion for us in the house of His ser - vant Da - vid: As He

spake by the mouth of His Ho - ly Pro - phets which have been since the world be -

- gan; That we should be sav - ed from our e - ne - mies, and from the

12

16

Evening Hymn

Te lucis ante terminum

7th century Ambrosian hymn

H. Balfour Gardiner (1877–1950)

18

* Soft reed. 4.8.16.

Defend_____ us from un - chas - ti - ty.
Ne pol - lu - an - tur cor - po - ra.

Gt. & Sw. with 16 ft.

men, a - men, a - men,
men, a - men, a - men,
dim.

men, a - men, a - men,
men, a - men, a - men,

men, a - men, a - men,
men, a - men, a - men,

a - - - men, a - men, a - men,
a - - - men, a - men, a - men,

a - - - men.
a - - - men.

a - - - men.
a - - - men.

a - - - men.
a - - - men.

a - - - men.
a - - - men.

How calmly the evening

T.T. Lynch (1818–71)

Edward Elgar (1857–1934)

10

prayer;___ O wing of the Lord, in Thy shel - ter be - friend -

prayer;___ O_ wing of the Lord, in Thy shel - ter be - friend -

prayer;___ O wing, O wing of the Lord, in Thy shel - ter be - friend -

still as a prayer;___ O wing of the Lord, in Thy shel - ter be - friend -

15

- ing,___ May we and our house - holds con - tin - ue to share.

- ing,___ May we and our___ house - holds con - tin - ue to share.

- ing,___ May we and our___ house - holds con - tin - ue to share.

- ing,___ May we and our___ house - holds con - tin - ue to share.

come, our life's work and its bre-vi-ty feel - ing,____

come, our__ life's__ work__ and its bre-vi-ty feel - -

come, our life's work__ and its bre-vi-ty feel - -

come, our life's work and its bre-vi-ty feel - -

____ With thanks for the past, for the fu-ture we pray.

- ing,____ With thanks for the past,__ for the fu-ture we pray.

- ing,____ With thanks for the past,__ for the fu-ture we pray.

- ing,____ With thanks for the past,__ for the fu-ture we pray.

Lord, save us from fol - ly; be with us in sor - row;_____ Su-stain us in

Lord, save us from fol - ly; be_____ with_____ us in sor - row; Su - stain_____ us in

Lord, save us from fol - ly; be_____ with us in sor - row; Su - stain_____ us in

Lord, save us from fol - ly; be with us in sor - row;_____ Su-stain us in

work till the time of our rest,_____ the time of our

work till the time_____ of our rest,_____ the time of our

work till the time_____ of our rest,_____ the time of our

work till the time_____ of our rest,_____ the time of our

I am Alpha and Omega

Revelation ch. 1, v. 8 and the Sanctus

John Stainer (1840–1901)

34

38

Jam sol recedit*
Now sinks the sun
from *St. Christopher*

St. Ambrose (340–97)
tr. Isabella G. Parker

Horatio W. Parker (1863–1919)

* The Chorus was originally written in the key of G flat, and should be sung in that key.
© Copyright 1900 Novello & Company Limited

Jerusalem on high
from *Hagar*

Samuel Crossman (1624–83)

F.A.G. Ouseley (1825–89)
ed. Heathcote Statham (1889–1973)

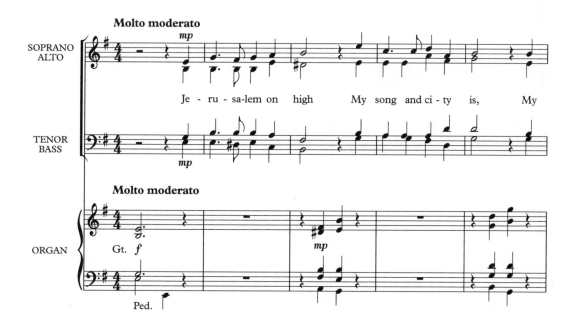

thi - ther guide the way: O hap - py

place! When shall I_____ be, My God, with_____

52

Thee, To____ see Thy____ Face?_____

Light out of darkness

from *The Light of Life, Op. 29*

Rev. Edward Capel-Cure (1860–1949)

Edward Elgar (1857–1934)
organ accompaniment arr. H.A. Chambers

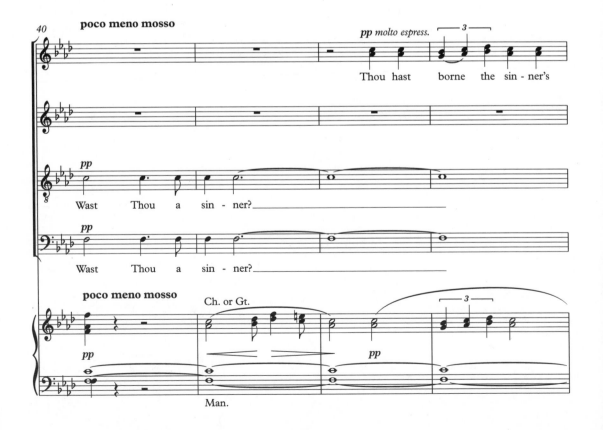

70

sor - row's sharp-set wreath.

sor - row's sharp - set wreath.

sor-row's sharp - set wreath.

mis - sion went.

Sw.

pp

Gt.

Sw.

Sw. to Ped.

poco meno mosso

73 S. pp

E-nough it was__ we need - ed Thee, our mi - se - ry__ a - lone did

Ch. or Gt.

pp

77 S.

pray, And Mer - cy an - swer'd ea - ger - ly,__ and trod for us__ steep Cal - va - ry's

A. pp

Mer - cy an - swer'd ea - ger - ly,__ and trod for us steep Cal - va - ry's

pp

Ch. or Gt.

The Lord is my shepherd

Psalm 23, vv. 1–4 and 6

S.S. Wesley (1810–76)

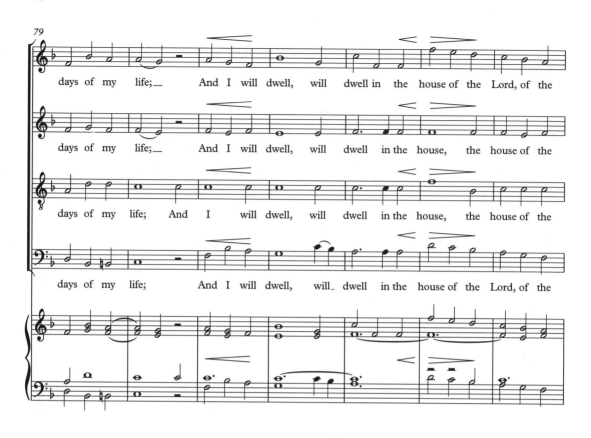

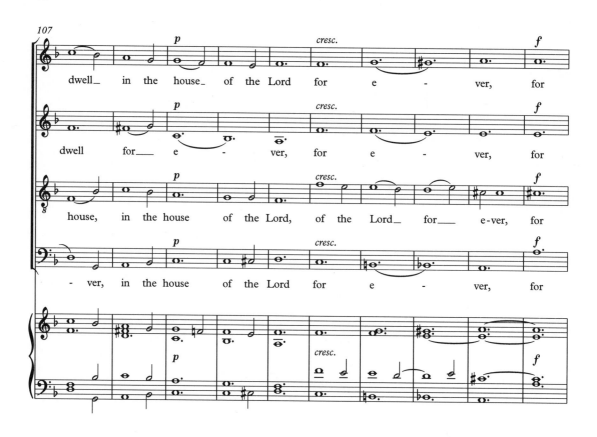

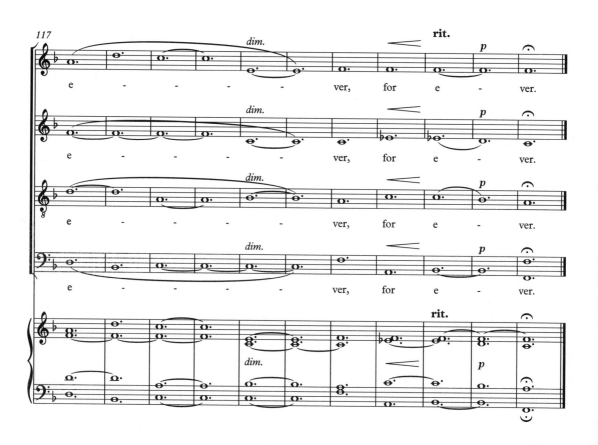

Love divine! all loves excelling

from *The Daughter of Jairus*

Charles Wesley (1707–88)   John Stainer (1840–1901)

down, Fix in us Thy hum-ble dwell-ing, all Thy faith-ful mer-cies crown.

Come, Al-migh-ty, to de-

Hast-en to re-turn and ne-ver, ne-ver-

-li-ver; let us all__ Thy grace re-ceive,

Magnificat and Nunc Dimittis in E

Magnificat

Canticle of Mary
St. Luke, ch. 1, vv. 46–55

John Goss (1800–80)

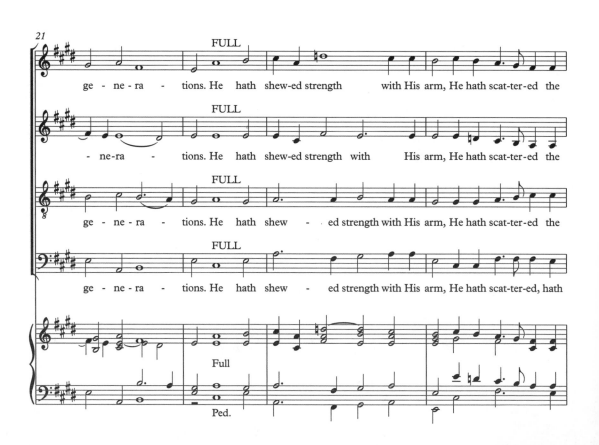

Nunc Dimittis

The Song of Simeon
St. Luke, ch. 2, vv. 29–32

O pray for the peace of Jerusalem

from *Praise the Lord, O my Soul*

Psalm 122, vv. 6–9

John Goss (1800–80)

O Saviour of the world

from The Visitation of the Sick
(Book of Common Prayer)

F.A.G. Ouseley (1825–89)
ed. Henry G. Ley (1887–1962)

-deem - ed us: Save_____ us and

-deem - ed us: Save_____ us and

-deem - ed us: Save us_____ and

-deem - ed us: Save_____ us and

Save us and help us,

Save_____ us_____ and help_____ us,

Save us and_____ help_____ us,

Save us and help us,

Remember me, O Lord

Psalm 106, vv. 4–5

G.A. Macfarren (1813–87)

See what love
from *St. Paul*

1 John ch. 3, v. 1

Felix Mendelssohn (1809–47)

110

love hath the Fa - ther be-stow'd on us in His good - ness.

- - ther be-stow'd on us in His good - ness.

love hath the Fa - ther be-stow'd on us in His good - ness.

- ther, hath the Fa - ther be-stow'd on us in His good - ness.

Seek ye the Lord

Isaiah ch. 55, vv. 6–7

J. Varley Roberts (1841–1920)

118

Sweet is Thy mercy

Rev. J.S.B. Monsell (1811–75)

Joseph Barnby (1838–96)

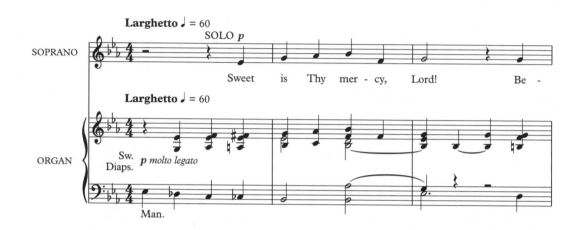

* cue size notes for rehearsal only

122

123

124

Teach me, O Lord

Psalm 119, vv. 33–34

John W. Gritton (1850–1928)

Turn Thy face from my sins

Psalm 51, vv. 9–11

Arthur Sullivan (1842–1900)

O holy night!
(Cantique de Noël)

Placide Cappeau
tr. based on the original by
J.S. Dwight (1813–93)

Adolphe Adam (1803–56)
arr. John E. West (1863–1929)

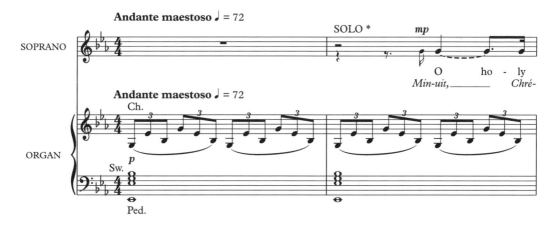

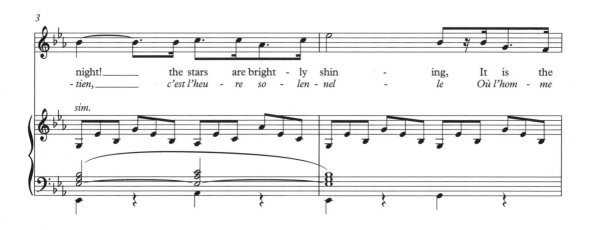

* or Tenor Solo

world___ in sin and er-ror pin — — ing, Till He ap-peared, and the soul felt its
-cer___ la tache o - ri - gi - nel - le Et de son père ar - rê - ter le cour-

worth. A thrill of hope, the wea - ry world re-joic - es, For
-roux. Le monde en - tier tres - sail - le d'es - pé-ran - ce A

yon - der breaks a new and glo - rious morn!___ Fall on your
cet - te nuit qui lui donne un sau - veur.___ Peu - ple à ge -

Led by the light___ of faith se - rene - ly beam - ing, With glow - ing
De no - tre foi___ que la lu - mière ar - den - te Nous gui - de

hearts by His cra - dle we stand; So, led by
tous au ber-ceau de l'en-fant. Comme au - tre-

light of a star sweet - ly gleam - ing, Here came the wise men___ from the O - rient
-fois, une é - toi - le bril-lan - te Y con - dui - sit les___ chefs de l'O - ri-